TWELVE LOOPS

TWELVE LOOPS
A System of Poems Without Metaphor

by J. A. Gucci

Student Edition

Poetic structure through paradox, repetition, and physical form.

Twelve short poems rooted in observable systems —designed for high school analysis, discussion, and creative response.

Pressure System Publishing

New York, New York

2026

**Twelve Loops: Poems Without Metaphor
(Student Edition)**
© 2026 J. A. Gucci
Published by Pressure System Press

All rights reserved.
No part of this publication may be reproduced or transmitted in any form or by any means, electronic or mechanical, without permission in writing from the publisher, except for brief quotations used in reviews or educational settings.

Printed in the United States of America

ISBN: 979-8-9946751-3-7

www.jagucci.com

Contents

Preface to the Reader.................... 7

Potoo Bird Breathing Loop
Voice / Self / Silence 9

Glacial Milk and Mist
Time / Moment / Eternity 10

Salt Flat and the Cactus
Matter / Mind / Being 11

Lake Reflection, Distortion
Image / Body / Absence 12

Word on Clay, Rift Echo
Word / Pattern / Break 13

Binary Code, Evolution, Glitch
Rule / Error / Form 14

Whisper Gallery
Signal / Interruption / Memory 16

Bee Sting, Still Curl
Obedience / Reflex / Sacrifice 17

Bark Explosion, Crown Shyness
Sacrifice / Limit / Grace 18

Summit That Isn't
Desire / Distance / End 19

Octopus Shifts Shape
Imitation / Echo / Transformation 20

Coffee Stirring Loop
Return / Trace / Begin 21

Afterword.................... 23
Composition Prompts.................... 24
Compositional Prompts 25
Reflection Questions 26
Structural Index 27
Glossary 28

Preface to the Reader

These twelve poems are built from real systems—
natural, mechanical, or behavioral.
There are no metaphors. Everything is what it is.
There are no narrators. No confessions. No
characters to sympathize with.

What loops, breaks, or changes is your job to notice.
You're not being told what it means. You're being
asked to see it happen.

Potoo Bird Breathing Loop

One-way loop,
shut eye.

Undulating branch—
steady,

snapped—
guttural shriek.

Still mouse twitching—
silent crickets.

Gray night-liver—
owl gaze.

Glacial Milk and Mist

Glacial milk,
a meandering stream—
cascade:

fresh water
fall—

salty ocean—
mist.

Salt Flat and the Cactus

Purple clouds drift
across the crusting ground—
water glaze.

Splayed—
pink pool
wooly cactus bloom—
I croon.

Steaming mud pots—
rock pillar.

Lake Reflection, Distortion

Teal toothed—
ragged spruce,
isosceles indigo—
fluted fir.

Bark beetle bores a hole—
turpentine air,
flitting crossbill—
puffed.

Glass lake—
natant needle—
ripples.

Word on Clay, Rift Echo

Croaks in a rift valley,
desert growls,
screech—

. . .

word—
scraped on clay,
uttered—

gasp
in the grassland.

Binary Code, Evolution, Glitch

0
1

This—
that.

01

This—
and that:

Awareness.

. . .

01
01

0101

pAtTeRn/ErOrR
TIME / change.

. . .

01101
01
000
01

Information:
reality.

E. v. o. l. U. T. I. O. N.

. . .

Exchange:
repeat:
exchange:
repeat:

render—
become.

Whisper Gallery

A whisper—
clung to jagged limestone

scattered—
blocked by a pillar—

secret.

Bee Sting, Still Curl

Style and lancet
rammed into hide.

Tattering wings—
twitching—

still curl.

Bark Explosion, Crown Shyness

Splattered rainbows
elongated shadows,

a trunk—
explodes.

Dead leaves,
hissing wind—

Spring—
shy crown.

Summit That Isn't

A crampon
rammed into ice,
rock—

lift,
heave,
breathless—

bent indigo skies,
a peak—

mid-slope.

Shape Shift

Undulating—
black-yellow arms,

splayed—
red-brown,

pulled together—
slate-grey.

Flat—
lionfish,
octopus.

Coffee Stirring Loop

Black topped
shimmering crema—
cream—

plunged deep,
billow back—
I stir:

rapid right circles,
laving left loops—

tan,
bronze.

Afterword

You've read twelve loops.

Each poem presents a system—something that
changes across a threshold.
Some changes are subtle. Some are abrupt.
Some return to where they began. Others don't.

If you read again, track the change more closely:
Where does it begin?
Where does it shift?
What is different after?

You may start to notice patterns across poems.
Not because they mean the same thing,
but because they move in similar ways.

These poems don't end in a final answer.
They hold a structure.

You can return to them,
and the structure will still be there—
even if what you notice changes.

Composition Prompts

Write Your Own Loop

Choose one of the following:

1. **The System Poem**
   Describe a real, observable process or transformation—natural or human-made. Don't explain what it means. Just show what it does.

2. **The Triad Poem**
   Choose 3 ideas in tension (e.g. wait / pressure / slip). Let your poem move through them without stating them directly.

3. **The Irreversible Loop**
   Begin with something simple.
   Show it change.
   End with something that looks like the beginning, but isn't.

Reflection Questions

Use these questions after reading or writing:

- What changes in the poem?
- Where is the turning point or shift?
- What is different at the end compared to the beginning?

- What repeats?
- What breaks or interrupts that pattern?

- Does the poem feel stable or unstable? Why?

- Which details help you see the change most clearly?

- If you the poem were longer, what would weaken it?
- If it were shorter, what might be lost?

Structural Index

Each poem in this book presents a system that changes across a threshold.

You can describe any poem using three parts:

- Beginning State — what is present at first
- Shift / Threshold — where change occurs
- Resulting State — what remains after

As you reread, try mapping each poem using this structure.

You may notice that different poems share similar patterns of change,
even when they describe different systems.

Glossary

Potoo Bird
A nocturnal bird found in Central and South America. It blends into tree branches during the day and is known for its still posture and sudden, loud call at night.

Glacial Milk
Cloudy water created by melting glaciers.
It contains fine rock particles that give it a pale, milky color.

Salt Flat
A wide, flat area covered with salt left behind after water evaporates.

Cactus
A plant that stores water and grows in dry environments, often with spines instead of leaves.

Reflection
An image seen in a surface (like water) where light bounces back.
Reflections can distort shape, color, and movement.

Rift Valley
A long, narrow valley formed when the Earth's crust pulls apart.

Binary Code
A system of information using only two values: 0 and 1.
It is the basic language of computers.

Glitch
A small error or unexpected change in a system.

Whisper Gallery
A space where sound travels along curved surfaces, allowing whispers to be heard clearly at a distance.

Lancet
A sharp, needle-like structure.
In bees, it is part of the stinger.

Crown Shyness
A pattern in some trees where the tops avoid touching each other, leaving visible gaps between branches.

Crampon
A metal device attached to a boot to help grip ice while climbing.

Crema
The light brown foam that forms on top of freshly brewed espresso.

Loop
A repeating process or motion.
In these poems, a loop may return to a similar state, but not exactly the same one.

System
A set of parts or actions that work together and change over time.

Shift
The point where something begins to change.

State
The condition something is in at a given moment.

Result
What remains after a change has taken place.

www.ingramcontent.com/pod-product-compliance
Lightning Source LLC
LaVergne TN
LVHW041644070526
838199LV00053B/3548